# 100 Views of the Golden Gate

Harold Davis

 **WILDERNESS PRESS** · BERKELEY, CA

100 Views of the Golden Gate

Copyright © 2008 by Harold Davis

Editor: Eva Dienel
Interior and cover design: Harold Davis and Phyllis Davis

*The Great Wave Off Kanagawa (Kanagawa oki nami-ura)* (page 13) and
*South Wind, Clear Sky (Gaifū kaisei)* (page 14) by Katsushika Hokusai (1760–1849),
used with permission by the British Museum.

Quote from Basho's *Narrow Road to the Interior* (page 10) and haiku (page 16) both translated from
the Japanese by Sam Hamill, Shambhala Publications.

The poem *The Mighty Task is Done* (page 148) by Joseph Baerman Strauss, chief engineer of the
Golden Gate Bridge, used courtesy of the Golden Gate Bridge Highway and Transportation District.

ISBN 978-0-89997-447-7

Manufactured in China

Published by:     Wilderness Press
                  1200 5th Street
                  Berkeley, CA 94710
                  (800) 443-7227
                  (800) 558-1696, fax
                  info@wildernesspress.com
                  www.wildernesspress.com

Library of Congress Cataloging-in-Publication Data

Davis, Harold, 1953-
  100 views of the Golden Gate / Harold Davis.
     p. cm.
  Includes bibliographical references.
  ISBN 978-0-89997-447-7 (hardcover)
  1. Golden Gate Bridge (San Francisco, Calif.)--Pictorial works. 2. Golden
Gate (Calif. : Strait)--Pictorial works. 3. San Francisco
(Calif.)--Pictorial works. I. Title. II. Title: One hundred views of the
Golden Gate.
  TG25.S225.D38 2008
  779'.9624.230979461--dc22

                    2007052377

# CONTENTS

# INTRODUCTION

During the late 18th and early 19th centuries, the great Japanese artist Katsushika Hokusai (1760–1849) wandered the largest Japanese island of Honshu. From these journeys, Hokusai created a series of woodblock prints titled *100 Views of Mount Fuji* that have come to symbolize Japan. Each of the Hokusai prints feature some aspect or representation of Mount Fuji. At no time in all the years that he spent wandering did Hokusai actually climb Mount Fuji.

Despite an artistic career that spanned 75 years, numerous genres, and changes in artistic fashion, *100 Views of Mount Fuji* remains Hokusai's best-known work.

Like the Japanese poet Matsuo Basho (1644–1694) whom Hokusai admired and emulated, Hokusai's spiral wanderings were a quest for perfection, spiritual as well as visual. Basho would write in his journal, "The moon and sun are eternal travelers. I have always been drawn by windblown clouds into dreams of a lifetime of wandering."

In Basho's footsteps, Hokusai journeyed the shores of Honshu, looking for Fuji beneath the crest of a great wave, in a spider's web, and through the bamboo. Hokusai found grist for his artist's mill everywhere and in everything, as long as Fuji was present. Wind and the great weather—representing spiritual perfection and spiritual conflict—were also part of the equation.

More than a decade ago, I left the grim cities of the Northeast for the promise of California and the Golden Gate. The Golden Gate is a symbol of California and the gateway to the Pacific. It is a bridge, a geographic place, and a state of mind.

When larger-than-life American explorer John Charles Fremont (1813–1890) first named the Golden Gate, the place was wild and only a hint of what was to come. The Ohlone tribal people gently trod the marshes round the bay and built their traditional shell mounds. Spanish missionaries pushed their way up the coast, and Russian fur traders came down from the Bering Strait to build crude wooden forts. The hustle and bustle of the quest for gold and modern life hadn't begun in this place. Even so, the Golden Gate was clearly special.

Miraculously, when the Golden Gate Bridge was built across the water from the Marin peninsula to the city of San Francisco in the 1930s, the result was a marvel of engineering and aesthetics that soared, endured, and framed the weather. Unlike many constructions, the bridge only added to the natural beauty of the area.

I began exploring San Francisco Bay, starting with the obvious—Lands End, the Marin Headlands, and the East Bay shore. Like Basho and Hokusai, my path would be spiral. Everywhere, I saw the Golden Gate. I returned often to favorite places to capture the best light and the weather, which rolled in across the towers of the bridge. My subject was not so much a bridge, or a place, but the spirit of the remarkable topography of water, weather, and light that blesses San Francisco Bay.

The best places to observe the Golden Gate are not easy to get to. For me, walking adds to the appeal. It's okay to drive, but a physical pilgrimage helps to reveal the essential spirit of a landscape.

For example, one balmy afternoon in late October, I studied the *San Francisco North Quadrant* USGS topographic map. This map shows (among other areas) the hills above Fort Baker outside Sausalito, and the northern side of the Golden Gate Bridge.

*The Great Wave Off Kanagawa (Kanagawa oki nami-ura),*
Katsushika Hokusai, 1760-1849

It seemed to me that there was a ridge that could be climbed by going up from above Fort Baker. You can tell on a topo map if something is steep by looking at the contour lines; the closer together the lines are, the steeper the slope is.

My hope was to find a location across from the northern end of the Golden Gate Bridge where I could photograph through both towers.

I picked up a friend, and we parked on Wolf Back Ridge Road, high above Sausalito. Technically, this is a private, no-trespassing area carved into the Marin Headlands section of the Golden Gate National Recreation Area.

We donned our hiking boots and backpacks, and scrambled down a steep hill to find the Coastal Trail. Heading south, we passed a high tension tower, and then trudged up the hill over the Waldo Tunnel. From

there, I could see straight down the ridge I had observed on the topo map.

The ridgeline ended on a rock platform. Yes, the towers of the bridge aligned perfectly from north to south. The setting sun lit the bridge from the west, and the waxing moon provided lighting from the other side.

I positioned my camera on the tripod, braced it with my camera backpack to keep it from vibrating in the wind, and exposed for 30 seconds. The time exposure turned the car headlights and tail lights into lines of light beneath the bridge (see the photos on pages 11 and 94).

Another time, I photographed from Lands End on the San Francisco side of the Golden Gate. Lands End is a rocky spur that juts into the Pacific Ocean on the outer side of the Golden Gate. You can look out to sea, across the Golden Gate to the rocky shores of the

*South Wind, Clear Sky (Gaifū kaisei)* by Katsushika Hokusai, 1760–1849

Marin Headlands, and toward land, through the Golden Gate Bridge, to San Francisco Bay.

The stone platform at Lands End, high above the waves, is home to a labyrinth, a circuitous path for peaceful walking meditations, created by Eduardo Aguilera (see the photo on page 83).

Coming back to the labyrinth on a windy day at spring solstice, I parked below the California Palace of the Legion of Honor. It was clear, but very windy and bitterly cold. I bundled into my cold-weather gear, and took the path through a golf course, home to many coyotes who watched me with close and solemn attention. Near the top of the stairs down to Lands End, I could hear the roar of surf in the wind.

I went down to the little rocky beach to the north and west of Lands End. It was a bit sheltered, and the waves were dancing higher and higher out beyond the cliffs, where the water caught the wind.

The sheer force embodied in these waves was enough to make anyone cautious. I kept my eye on the pounding wa-ter, and kept my equipment on my back for a quick retreat.

From one angle, looking around the rocky corner below Lands End, I was surprised to see part of the Golden Gate Bridge. Then, a giant breaker headed for the shore, appearing to tower over the bridge.

I got down on my belly and took the photo on page 12 of the wave crashing around, under, and visually above the bridge (Lands End is on the right).

For me, photography is a quest in the knight-errant sense. If I take on a photographic quest, I am going on an adventure. I never know in advance what the adventure will bring, but it is always wise to be prepared for the unexpected. It is truly the journey, and not the destination, that counts.

Like Hokusai, who created art that used Mount Fuji as its crucial icon but who never in all his wanderings ascended the mountain, I have not photographed *from* the Golden Gate Bridge.

I've used the Golden Gate as my excuse, my "MacGuffin," for exploring parts of San Francisco Bay that interest me.

I've stood on Mission Peak above San Jose, probably the highest mountain in the Bay Area that you can climb only by foot, and watched the fog slither in past the Golden Gate far to the north.

Directly across from the Golden Gate, I've observed sunset and sunrise from the summit of Tilden Park's Wildcat Peak, with its wraparound vistas of the San Francisco Bay, San Pablo Bay, the Straits of Carquinez, and Mount Diablo.

I've spent afternoons and evenings on Indian Rock in Berkeley, waiting for the perfect light, weather, and position of the sun. Sometimes I'm the only one on Indian Rock, and at other times there's a whole party with kids, dogs, and musicians.

About 1,000 vertical feet down from the summits of the Coastal Range to the shore, I have visited the East Bay marshes at the fringes of the tidal waters, where the towers of the bridge peak above the Marin hills. It's hard to photograph in and around the tidal marshes without getting splashed with mud.

The vistas from the beaches of the inner Golden Gate—Horseshoe Bay, Kirby Cove, Baker Beach, China Beach, Point Diablo, and Point Bonita—have been mine to know and love in summer and winter, spring and fall, at sunset and after sunset, by moonlight and starlight.

Depending on which source you believe, Hokusai's *100 Views of Mount Fuji* actually had either 104 or 110 views. The point is, it was never the precise number of views.

One hundred views is a starting place for *seeing*. It is one hundred ways to see the Golden Gate, one hundred starting places to adventures that lead to clarity of vision.

Any view of the Golden Gate, like any view of Mount Fuji, always involves the weather. Basho put it like this in a haiku:

*Chilling autumn rains*
*curtain Mount Fuji, then make it*
*more beautiful to see*

The weather is itself a moving show. The fog sits in a great cloud bank out to sea to the west of the Golden Gate. Like a great bellows in the evening, the fog blows in and covers San Francisco Bay with tiny, nitrogen-rich water droplets.

The natural bellows send the weather up the bay, through the Straits of Carquinez, then up the Sacramento River delta to California's great Central Valley. In the early hours of the day, the action reverses.

Over time, watching this weather action is like observing a theatrical curtain. It's not clear whether the play happens before or after the curtain is dropped or raised, but it is certain that without the interplay of light, fog, and weather, there would be much less beauty. Partial obscurity makes for mystery and majesty.

And without my wanderings, I wouldn't be able to capture this beauty of the Golden Gate that I love so much. For Hokusai, Mount Fuji was sacred—which may partly explain the spiritual quality of many of the woodblock prints that comprise *100 Views of Mount Fuji*.

I hope I've conveyed a similar sense that the wonders of the Golden Gate are simple but profound. The more you look, and the more you wander, the more you see.

*Harold Davis*

Berkeley, CA

# Peerless Bay

On the storm-bound coast of Northern California, there is one great natural harbor. Surrounded by sacred mountains, beautiful beyond compare, there is one focus of this peerless bay—the Golden Gate.

The light here is ever changing. The modes of the weather are like whims of heaven. The city on the bay looks out on the Golden Gate.

Gauge for incoming weather, beacon of hope for the lost and for those seeking a new life, both symbol and practicality: The Golden Gate is written upon the face of the land and upon the people who live there. Entrance, exit, hope, finality, crossing, bridge, landscape, passage-by-sea, promise of prosperity and a new life—the Golden Gate is all this and more for those who are lucky enough to live within its penumbra.

San Francisco Bay is an estuary. The city is built around tidal marshes, home to abundant wildlife.

Some facts: Water originating as snowmelt in the Sierra Nevada, and accounting for about 40 percent of the water drainage in California, flows down the Sacramento and San Joaquin rivers.

Both rivers flow through the Sacramento River delta into Suisun Bay, then through the Straits of Carquinez into San Pablo Bay. At San Pablo Bay, the rivers are joined by the Napa River, flowing from the north; at its south end, San Pablo Bay flows into San Francisco Bay. Usually, this entire system of interconnected bays is called San Francisco Bay.

San Francisco Bay covers about 1,600 square miles (this includes the connected bays, as well as wetlands and intertidal zones). At its widest—facing the Golden Gate—San Francisco Bay extends about 12 miles.

Generally, San Francisco Bay is pretty shallow. Originally, freshwater wetlands transitioned to salt marshes and tidal mud flats, with a deep channel following the ancient course of the river that helped make the bay in geologic times.

The dredging for gold up the Sacramento and San Joaquin rivers sent tremendous piles of silt down into the San Francisco Bay in the 1800s. The U.S. Army Corps of Engineers' efforts to create and maintain deep-water shipping in the channels to the great Port of Oakland and up the Sacramento River led to changes in the floor of the bay (and the extension of Yerba Buena Island to create Treasure Island). So, today San Francisco Bay comprises a shallow estuarine environment that also includes deep-water navigation channels. Under water as well as above water, this is a topography of variety.

The Golden Gate is the only nautical approach to the only natural harbor for hundreds of miles. It is one of the great natural harbors of the world. Since the time of the Spaniards, the Golden Gate has been guarded with fortresses. These battlements, however, have seldom been called upon to do anything but stand guard.

Fort Point, on the south side of the Golden Gate, stood before there was a bridge. Taking Fort Point from the Spanish was a signal of the independence of California before it joined the United States.

Below Fort Point lies a small beach under the lee of huge boulders that protect against erosion. At sunset, I clambered down over these large, slick boulders. My photograph on the facing page shows the shallows of the bay sloping down to the untold depth of a deep-water channel, with the Golden Gate Bridge and Marin Headlands behind, and a light mist rising over the water.

The homes and gardens on the east side of San Francisco Bay cling to the steep sides of the Coastal Range like—as former mayor of Oakland, Jerry Brown, once put it—"Italian hill town architecture." Actually, the East Bay hills have a style all their own: at once lush, opulent, but surprisingly informal. Networks of footpaths make it easy to walk up and down stairs, some elegant and some crumbling beneath the aggressive flora of the region. Roads are so convoluted, steep, and twisty that finding destinations, and getting back out again, can be like working through a maze.

Berkeley, Kensington, and parts of Oakland directly face the Golden Gate. From the homes in the hills in these cities, you can look straight across at the Golden Gate, as shown in the photo here. Looking straight at the Golden Gate, you can see downtown San Francisco on the left (to the south), linked with the sparkling lights of the East Bay "flats" by the Bay Bridge (which passes through Yerba Buena).

Directly in front of the southern tower of the Golden Gate Bridge, East Bay residents can see Alcatraz. To the north (and right) of the Golden Gate are the hills of the Marin Headlands, reaching up to their summit with Mount Tamalpais.

Below the flats of Berkeley, the Berkeley Pier stretches into the bay, looking for all the world as though it would cross the bay if only it were complete. This, however, is an illusion.

Lucky are those who live across from the Golden Gate. The lines of light stretch out to a Pacific sunset every evening when the bay isn't covered in fog or rain clouds. Sipping drinks in the living room, watching the show from a terrace or hot tub, one can gauge the incoming weather for the next day and believe it is possible to live in an earthly paradise!

Berkeley's fishing pier is a crumbling reminder of the magnificence and fun of the bay. It was built in 1926 to extend 3.5 miles into the bay as a ferry dock (it was part of U.S. 40 before the Bay Bridge opened).

Today, portions of the pier go out 2.5 miles, but you can walk out only a little more than half a mile before you come to an abrupt barricade.

Walking out on the Berkeley Pier at sunset is a feast for the senses. You are surrounded by the sights, sounds, and smells of the bay, with a view directly facing the Golden Gate. With luck, the breezes will caress, and as the lights of the pier come on, you will find yourself in a jeweled and magical world.

To sail by the
Golden Gate—a
fresh breeze behind
and a red sunset
blazing ... that
is paradise!

Far above the East Bay cities, the crest of the Coastal Range is park land. Open spaces ring the bay, and Wildcat Peak in Tilden Park provides a bird's-eye view of the Golden Gate, as shown in the photograph to the right.

To take this photo, I hiked up to Wildcat Peak in winter, when the air was clearest. The golden light of sunset made a glorious panorama of the bay and Golden Gate.

Then the show was done and the lights began to come on. With a bitter wind behind me, I hiked through the darkness toward home and into civilization.

Dungeness crab, halibut, and Pacific salmon use San Francisco Bay as a nursery.

The bay is part of the Pacific Flyway. Literally millions of waterfowl pass through the mud flats at the fringes of San Francisco Bay every year. Several endangered birds are found in the tidal marshes of San Francisco Bay and nowhere else.

For all this teeming diversity of wildlife and beauty of the bay shoreline, this coast is surprisingly neglected. The city of Albany's waterfront park is built on landfill, and much of the rubbish from the garbage dump days still remains. In many places, multilane freeways line the shore. Simply getting to the shoreline can involve ingenuity.

I wish I could see the bay as once it was, when the way to navigate was to flit from grassy marsh to grassy marsh in a light kayak.

But even as an industrialized corruption of what it once was, the shoreline of San Francisco Bay has a certain purity, and an immense beauty.

Near Point Isabel, I wandered down onto the stinky tidal flats, oozing with mud, and photographed the teeming wildfowl with the bridge as a backdrop.

SACRED WEATHER

The weather of San Francisco Bay is notoriously unpredictable. "Don't like the weather?" old-timers ask, with the punch line: "Then wait five minutes."

For me, this changeability translates into constant doubt and the need for patience. The Bay Area weather gods are fickle and don't reveal their secrets lightly. I can start for a destination, camera and tripod on my back, under crystalline skies. By the time I've arrived, the Golden Gate is covered with dense fog and there's nothing to photograph.

Conversely, the skies can be cloudy, covered in shades of pearl gray. Darkness of oncoming night seems to settle in. Then, for a brief moment before the light fails, the sun shines through, creating a memorable pattern of light and shadow behind the Golden Gate. If I'm not already in position, heedless of the drizzle, then I've missed the moment.

On the night of a full June moon, I was looking east at the Golden Gate Bridge, while the moon illuminated the wisps of fog, creating the festive look seen in the photo on the facing page.

A red sky at sunset, projecting onto the high clouds surrounding the Golden Gate, brings rumor of incoming storms.

The arch of cloud over the Golden Gate, lit with a powerful glow, is a light show for anyone present to see it, and a reminder of the sacred weather of the Golden Gate.

The mountains of San Francisco Bay and the influence of the Pacific Ocean produce a region of microclimates. It can be cold, wet, and windy on top of a ridge, and almost tropical with a balmy breeze only a few feet away.

The bay's moist, mild winters and dry summers are part of a rare Mediterranean climate shared only with the southwestern shores of Africa, the west coast of Chile, parts of Australia, and, of course, portions of the Mediterranean basin.

Good days for photography come almost anytime, but least often in the summer. Rain falls from December through March, so to see the Golden Gate in the rain, come here in the winter.

Summer brings the most fog. If the fog doesn't persist all day, it may burn off on the bay side of the city of San Francisco by the middle of the day. The Golden Gate Bridge can be the front line in the battle between the sun and the fog, with the wind playing an auxiliary role, first allied with the sun, and then on the side of the fog.

When the fog is banished from the Golden Gate, it often returns with the late-afternoon breezes, filling the Golden Gate and San Francisco Bay with a thick, white blanket a few hours after sunset, starting the weather cycle anew.

Autumn brings the warmest days of the whole year, along with days and evenings of incredible clarity. This time of year tends to see multiday cycles.

After a week of mostly fog-filled days, there's a break in the weather, perhaps accompanied by light showers. The next autumn day is crystal clear and wonderful. It seems as though you can reach across the bay and grab the Golden Gate in the palm of your hand.

Over the next few days, the atmosphere gradually becomes a little murkier. Finally, a day that is entirely clouds and fog comes. And so, the sacred weather cycle starts again.

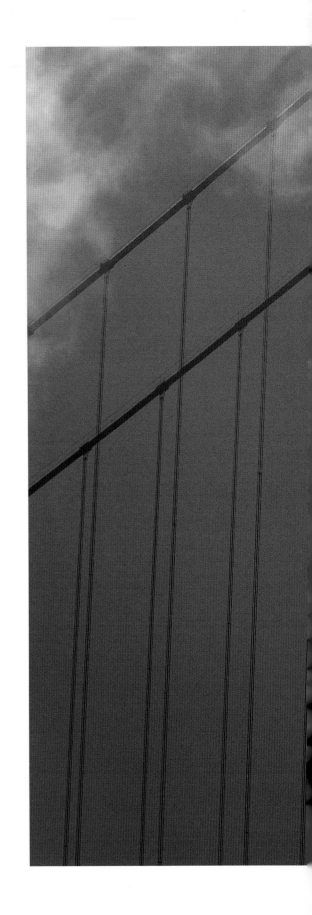

When you think of a shadow, probably a dark projection on the ground is what comes to mind: for example, your figure rendered as a black shadow by an oblique sun. But shadows can also contain color, and they do not have to be projected on the ground.

The shadows of the Golden Gate Bridge towers, shown on pages 72 and 73, are projected on the fog.

Technically, a light source like the sun casts a two-part shadow, the dark umbra in the center of the shadow and the lighter penumbra at the shadow's edges. The shadow you might see projected on a sidewalk is mostly umbra, while the shadows of the Golden Gate Bridge towers are largely penumbra.

The shadow projected on the fog is closer than the bridge, so the shadows appear larger than life, magnifying the size of the actual bridge.

Many times, the Golden Gate is shrouded in fog or weather clouds. It's never the same twice. In the evening, a soft, slick mist of fog may roll through the Golden Gate.

Observers (and commuters) know that sometimes the entire bridge is shrouded in fog, sometimes one tower is in the clear, sometimes the other is, and sometimes wisps of fog race through the Golden Gate.

It's exhilarating, mesmerizing, and mysterious to observe and try to predict. If you are driving across the bridge, will bright sunshine dominate, or will you be alone in a world of mist and fog? If you are climbing the ridges of the Marin Headlands for a special view of the Golden Gate, will you get a sun bath or stand drenched and chilled to the bone with droplets of fog catching on your clothes?

From Wildcat Peak across the bay, clouds roll in through the Golden Gate as shown in the photo on the right. Nothing ever stays the same, and from one instant to the next, the painterly views and vistas are revealed, and then hidden and gone forever.

# Threading the Golden Gate

These are dangerous waters. Currents are strong, and fog often hides the hazards. There's a great variety in the depth of the channels, and barely submerged rocks stretch from the Farallon Islands into the Golden Gate channel itself. Until 1930, a partially submerged rock in the middle of the Golden Gate passage stood between the shores where the Golden Gate Bridge now soars. This hazard to navigation was blasted away as part of the bridge construction process.

In 1853, the steamship *Independence* was lost, with 300 passengers aboard, when the captain mistook rocks for some whales. Also in 1853, the steamer *Tennessee* was lost near Point Bonita, fortunately with no loss of life. The passengers safely drifted ashore to a deserted Marin cove, now known as Tennessee Beach.

In 1854, the clipper ship *San Francisco*, inbound from New York, struck the rocks on the north side of the Golden Gate opposite Fort Point.

The litany of shipwrecks and disasters related to the fierce maritime environment of the Golden Gate goes on and on, into modern times.

The path to beauty often travels through danger. The perils that make the Golden Gate so dangerous also make this coast beautiful—one might say, perilously beautiful. Strong, erratic currents combine with gale-force winds, low and intermittent visibility, and a coast with dramatic jagged cliffs and glorious sand beaches.

Just think! On the south side of the Golden Gate, starting with the dramatic and wild landscape of Lands End, you have China Beach, Baker Beach, and the drama of Helmet Rock and the Fort Point Rocks.

Under what is now the bridge, Fort Point guards the Golden Gate.

Curving into San Francisco Bay, you'll find Crissy Field, Anita Rock, and the wharfs of Fort Mason.

On the northern shore of the Golden Gate, the inner approach to the bay is guarded by Fort Baker, situated on Point Cavullo and Horseshoe Bay.

The northern buttresses of the Golden Gate Bridge are built on the rocks called the Needles and Lime Point.

Continuing north, Kirby Cove is nestled, a beautiful sand gem between rock walls, as seen in the photo on pages 40 and 41.

To get to the beach at Kirby Cove, you walk down a dirt road (that is closed to cars) from the parking lot next to the old fortifications above the bridge.

I love to stay past sunset at Kirby Cove to photograph. There's no problem walking back up the dirt road at night, but if you do stay after the sun goes down at Kirby Cove, beware of the treacherous waters of the Golden Gate. The tide can come up extremely fast, and much of the beach is under water at high tide.

Past Kirby Cove, the topography gets steeper until the aptly named Point Diablo is rounded.

The bay between Point Bonita and Point Diablo is called Bonita Cove, and is home to the wonderful and secluded Black Sands Beach. If you ever get the chance to wander this beach, a short, three-quarter-mile walk down from the road, do it! It's likely you'll see no one else on this entire stretch of beach, and you'll be amazed you are so close to a major city.

Beyond Point Bonita is the outer Golden Gate, stretching from the rugged Marin Headlands across to the city lights of South San Francisco, as seen in the photo on page 110.

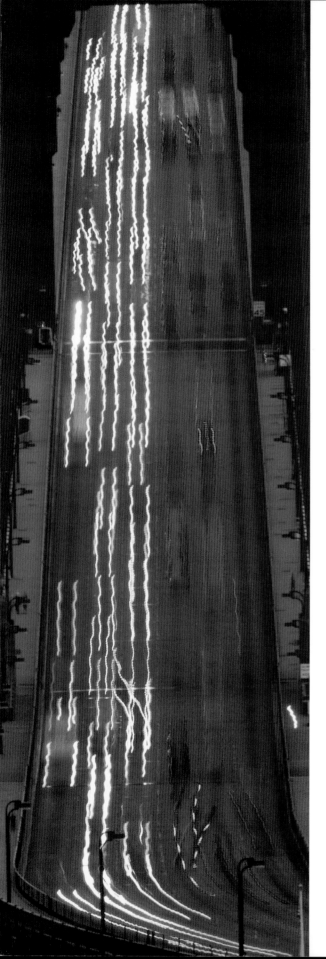

Looking down the line of cliff
at high tide, shadow of bridge
behind, where is the refuge on
this rocky shore?

Coming up the trail from Kirby Cove, it was fully night. Not a pitch-black night, because there was a sliver of moon and light pollution from the bridge and city. But it was as dark as it was going to get.

Up on the fortifications of the Marin Headlands, I decided to see how long a time exposure I could make of the Golden Gate Bridge.

First, I did some tests to get the exposure right. As I mentioned, this wasn't a pitch-black night, and the bridge was pretty lit up, so it seemed that eight minutes would be about the longest I could go.

I used a "bulb" setting on my camera (which holds the shutter open as long as it is depressed) and a programmable remote device to do the "pressing." You can set this thing to any amount of time you'd like, even hours and hours. A headlamp really comes in handy for setting electronics in the dark.

You need a great deal of patience for this kind of exposure, particularly in cold and dark conditions. Even with a fast digital memory card, each exposure took roughly 50 percent of the shutter speed time for writing to the card before I could use the camera again. This meant at least 12 minutes of standing around in the cold and dark for each exposure!

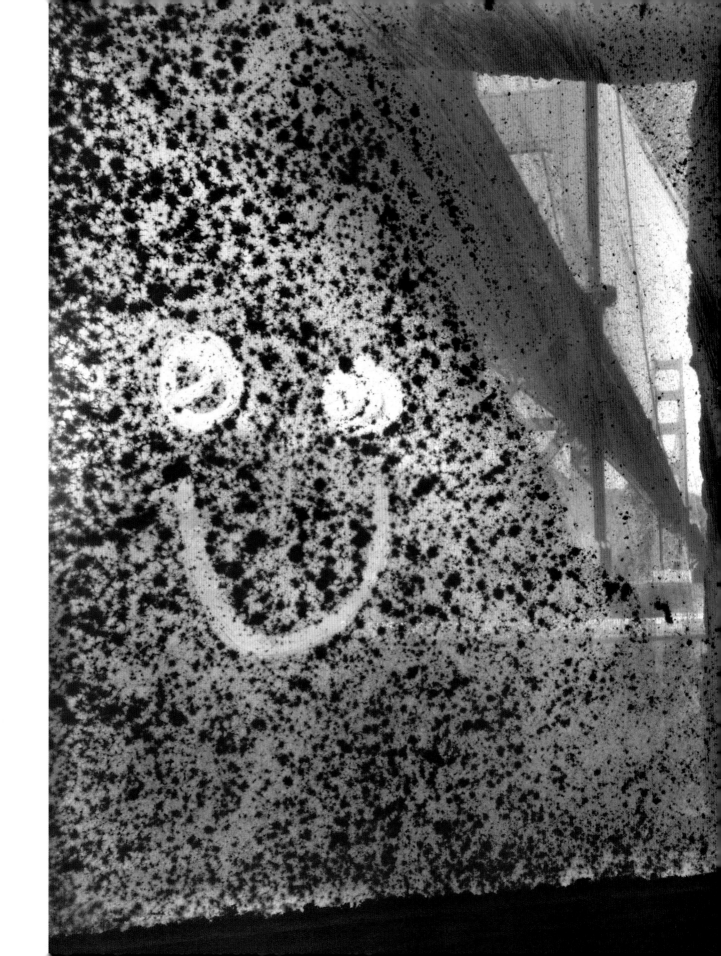

SETTING SUN

Photographers and people who like to observe the changing landscape know that there is nothing more important than light. Learning to pay attention to light is very important. What's the direction of the light? In other words, where is the source of the light, and what is it illuminating? More subjectively, what is the intensity of the light? Does the light create shadows? Does the light have special qualities?

Tracking the sun is part of this job of observing light and the landscape. That's easy, you say, the sun rises in the east and sets in the west. Well, that's not quite all there is to it.

In fact, there are only a few times each year when the sun rises exactly due east and sets exactly due west.

Sunset, the point at which the sun hits the western horizon, varies from north to south: from summer solstice (north) to winter solstice (south). The north-to-south direction depends on the hemisphere; if you live in the southern hemisphere, the direction is south to north.

At the equinoxes, the sun is smack-dab in the middle of its setting range from north to south along the western horizon. The extent of the north-to-south range, and the daily difference between setting points, is determined by latitude (how far north or south you are).

This becomes relevant if you want to photograph the Golden Gate at sunset.

Photographs of sunset behind the Golden Gate are usually better when the sun is behind (or not that far from either side) of the bridge. This happens twice during the annual migration of sunset points, roughly in November and February.

There's a fairly complex geometry of geography at work. First, as I explained, you need to track the western sun against the Golden Gate, taking into account the sun's journey along the western horizon from solstice to solstice.

Next, you need to understand the position of the observer (or photographer), because this changes the relationship of the sun to the Golden Gate. Assuming you are standing to the east of the Golden Gate, perhaps on the other side of San Francisco Bay, the farther south your observation point, the farther north the setting sun intersects the Golden Gate Bridge. Conversely, the farther north you are standing, the farther south is this apparent intersection point.

Relative elevation also changes things. The higher your elevation to the east (perhaps you've climbed Wildcat Peak in the Coastal Range), the later the sun sets. If you're high up, the sun doesn't appear to set right into the Golden Gate Bridge, but instead to the rear of it. As the sun moves in its path toward the horizon, the point where it falls beneath the horizon will probably be more off center than from a lower observation point.

The relationship of astronomical geometry to the Golden Gate is only a starting place, of course. Qualitative aspects of light come into play when atmospheric conditions such as fog, mist, and weather join the production.

Let the day fade into night, the sunset to moonrise! The geometry of the moon in relation to the Golden Gate Bridge works pretty much the way the sun and bridge relationship does, biased to the perfection of the moon's own phases. In other words, there are probably only one or two days per year when it's possible to get a good view of the moon rising to the east of the bridge.

On the deserted beach at Kirby Cove, day fades to night with stars' pinpoints in the sky.

A mist rises off the waters of the Golden Gate as the air chills.

One by one, the lights of the bridge come on in staggered sequence. By then, the lights of San Francisco are vibrant and saturated beneath the Golden Gate Bridge.

At night, the Golden
Gate is truly golden!

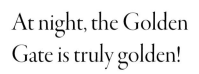

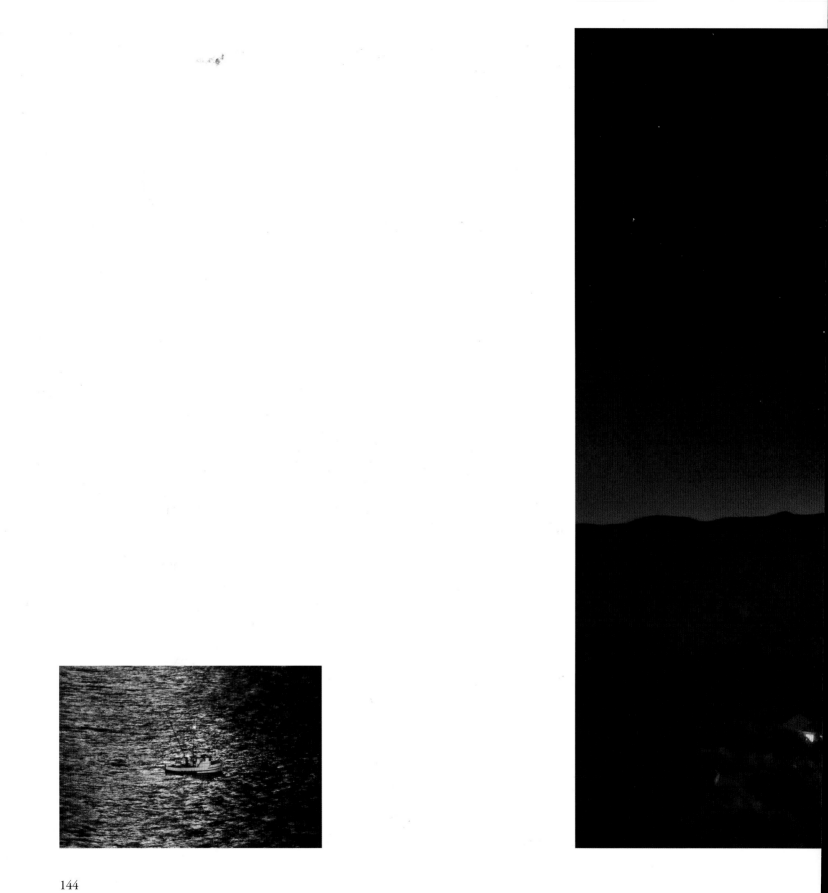

**The Mighty Task Is Done**


At last the mighty task is done;
Resplendent in the western sun;
The Bridge looms mountain high
On its broad decks in rightful pride,
The world in swift parade shall ride
Throughout all time to be.


Launched midst a thousand hopes and fears,
Damned by a thousand hostile sneers.
Yet ne'er its course was stayed.
But ask of those who met the foe,
Who stood alone when faith was low,
Ask them the price they paid.
High overhead its lights shall gleam,
Far, far below life's restless stream,
Unceasingly shall flow....


*—Joseph Baerman Strauss,*
*creator of the Golden Gate Bridge*

NOTES ABOUT THE PHOTOGRAPHY

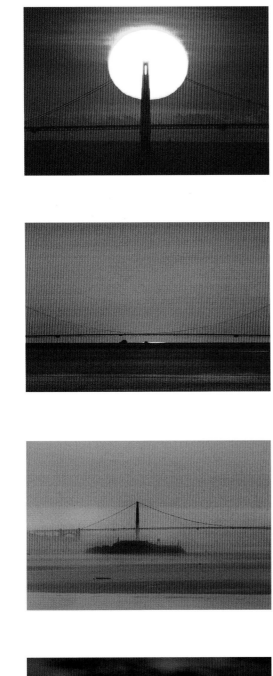

**1**

Many days of observation and planning paid off with this photo of the sun almost centered behind the southern tower of the Golden Gate Bridge.

I took this photo from Indian Rock in Berkeley using a long telephoto lens and a tripod. To protect my eyes, I primarily reviewed images in the LCD (rather than the camera's viewfinder). When I did need to look directly, I peered through a special piece of welder's glass. *(Photo on front cover.)*

**2**

When the sun dipped below the western horizon, it seemed to me that the horizon line was a hard edge. In other words, the world was flat, and the ships in this photo, if they headed west, would drop off the edge.

I processed this photo to emphasize the "world is flat" effect by bringing out texture and noise in the water, but I left the bridge and sky relatively smooth. *(Photo on title page.)*

**3**

This is a photo from Panoramic Hill, which is partly in Berkeley and partly in Oakland. From high up Panoramic Hill, you get oblique views of the Golden Gate, with the island of Alcatraz visually shoved in front of the southern bridge span. On this day, the sun was setting in fiery reds and yellows. I had time for one tripod-mounted telephoto shot before the colors faded and the world of the Golden Gate turned back into haze. *(Photo on pages 4 and 5.)*

**4**

From Wildcat Peak in Tilden Park, there's a nearly panoramic view. One of the few mountain summits in the Bay Area that can be reached only on foot, this aerie looks down and across the lower hills in the Coastal Range, toward the Golden Gate.

What a great place to watch the play of clouds, weather, and sunset! *(Photo on page 6.)*

You can photograph a classic view of the Golden Gate from the Marin Headlands fortifications just to the north, and slightly west, of the bridge. This photo is from one of the most accessible fortifications, Battery Spencer.

It pays to wait for sunset, or a little after. When the angle of the sun is right, and the fog is not too heavy, golden light sweeps through the aptly named Golden Gate. *(Photo on pages 8 and 9.)*

5

Lucky is the Marin resident who commutes to work across the Golden Gate! But, you say, rush hour is rush hour, and being stuck in traffic is being stuck.

True, but if I *had* to be stuck in traffic, where would be more magnificent than on the Golden Gate Bridge on a lovely evening?

I photographed the bridge at rush hour from a ridge to the southwest of Sausalito. *(Photo on page 11.)*

6

At Lands End, the corner of the Pacific Ocean and the Golden Gate, vast, wind-driven waves meet a rocky shore. If you walk the shoreline here, you should always keep one eye out for rogue waves.

For this photo, I lay with my belly in a tide pool and waited until a large breaker appeared to top the northern tower of the Golden Gate Bridge. *(Photo on pages 12 and 13.)*

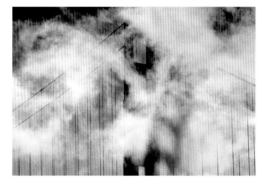

7

A strong projection of a shadow on a cloud—like the one shown in this photograph—is an unusual atmospheric phenomenon called a "crepuscular" effect. For the most part, to witness something like this, you'd have to live in Gotham City and observe Batman's signal. Crepuscular rays are more common around the Golden Gate than almost anywhere else in the world—but are still rare even here. *(Photo on page 15.)*

8

**9**

On its northern approach to the Golden Gate Bridge, the U.S. 101 freeway passes through Waldo Tunnel. To take this photo, I found my way to the mound high above Waldo Tunnel.

From the mound, hundreds of feet above the tunnel roof, the lights of San Francisco and the Golden Gate spread out before me, and the car lights on the roadways approaching the bridge cast a fiery glow. *(Photo on pages 16 and 17.)*

**10**

I was standing on a small bluff toward the western end of Kirby Cove. First, the lights of San Francisco came on. Then, gradually, the lights of the Bay Bridge appeared. (The Bay Bridge is seen in this photo under the Golden Gate Bridge.)

Finally, the lights of the Golden Gate Bridge itself appeared, and I was pleased to take this photo that includes the night lights of both bridges. *(Photo on pages 18 and 19.)*

**11**

In stormy weather, the view of the outer Golden Gate must have been terrifying to early pilgrims.

I took this photograph of the Marin coast to the north of the entrance to the Golden Gate during a storm. Rain was driving hard. I stood in the partial shelter of Battery Mendell, one of the decaying forts that still guard the shore at the entrance to the Golden Gate. *(Photo on page 19.)*

**12**

I was positioned on the fortifications that are behind and back from the beach at Kirby Cove. As the moon rose behind the Golden Gate Bridge, the scene with the lit clouds looked to me like a magnificent painting by J.M.W. Turner.

I exposed a series of time exposures of the moon rising. The length of the exposures flattened the surf and enhanced the colors in the sky. *(Photo on pages 20 and 21.)*

This is a midsummer view of the bay and Golden Gate at twilight from near the Lawrence Hall of Science. The sun had set and turned the world of San Francisco Bay pink with the haze of summer. *(Photo on pages 22 and 23.)*

**13**

I reached the wharf to the southeast of Fort Point on the San Francisco side of the Golden Gate in time for sunset.

Clambering down the large, slick boulders that border a pocket beach, I set my tripod at the edge of the surf to photograph the Golden Gate Bridge with the Marin Headlands in the rear. *(Photo on page 25.)*

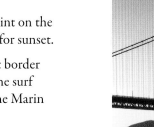

**14**

I was making one of my frequent afternoon pilgrimages to Indian Rock in Berkeley to honor sunset. When I got to Indian Rock, rain was coming down hard. I gritted my teeth, pulled on a jacket, and climbed the slippery steps up the rock. After a while, the rain stopped. Just at sunset, the wind picked up, and a huge, but intermittent, bank of clouds scuttled across the horizon. In the glow of clouds, I quickly snapped a series of photos before the weather closed in again. *(Photo on pages 26 and 27.)*

**15**

The sun had set, the lights of the bridge and the city had come on, and it was getting cold. I stayed on top of Indian Rock for a last photo that showed the contrast between the sunset colors in the sky and the city lights that were appearing below. *(Photo on page 27.)*

**16**

**17**

From the parapet on the edge of the terrace at the Lawrence Hall of Science in the East Bay hills, San Francisco Bay spreads out from south to north. I used multiple exposures on a panoramic tripod head to create this stitched together version of the bay. When I put the separate photos together, I decided to leave some of the lines between the images (rather than blending the images seamlessly). My idea was to create an old-fashioned panorama that might have been stitched together with tape and accordion folds. *(Photo on pages 28 and 29.)*

**18**

I photographed this view from the roof of an opulent East Bay home on Thanksgiving Day as the sun set and a turkey roasted.

The angle of view in this vista interested me, especially the way the lights along University Avenue in Berkeley seemed to point almost directly at the Golden Gate. *(Photo on pages 30 and 31.)*

**19**

After the sun sets, and as the street lights come on, the Berkeley Pier is often deserted, except for stray photographers and fishermen.

With this photo, I liked the way the lights looked against the sky, and the contrast between the dark pier and the orange sunset. *(Photo on page 32.)*

**20**

Another photo from the Berkeley Pier, on this evening, the water, pier, and bridge shimmered and glowed with golden light. Once again, the pier was almost deserted, except for the shadow figure of someone out for a walk, captured with the time-lapse photography. *(Photo on pages 32 and 33.)*

When you walk as far as you can go on the Berkeley Pier, you end up against these boards. If you look through the slats, you can see the ruins of the pier stretching farther and the Golden Gate Bridge off in the distance.

My photo was framed to get in focus both the background scene and the boards, tagged with colored graffiti. *(Photo on page 34.)*

21

In this photo from Panoramic Hill in Berkeley, the Bay Area is spread out below like jewels in the night. It's amazing to me how the different color temperatures of the various lights at night create a glow, or haze of light, above the city and bay. *(Photo on pages 34 and 35.)*

22

Guests were coming to dinner, and I didn't have much time. I drove over to Indian Rock, about 10 minutes away. It was getting darker. I had trouble finding a parking place.

On top of the rock, someone called cheerily, "You are 10 minutes too late!"

I set up my tripod and telephoto lens, and took a few photos. In my mind, it was perfect timing, since I was home in time for the dinner guests! *(Photo on pages 36 and 37.)*

23

This is a photo from the front porch of a home perched high up, at the intersection of Michigan Avenue and Kentucky Avenue in the Berkeley hills.

How vast the sky looked in this landscape of water, city, Golden Gate, and coastal mountains! *(Photo on page 38.)*

24

**25**

Beside San Francisco Bay, the water can often seem tranquil. The extent of this breakwater, adjacent to the Berkeley Marina in Cesar Chavez Park, shows that this tranquility is often an illusion, and that cities opposite the Golden Gate need to be prepared for volatile weather. *(Photo on page 39.)*

**26**

On the beach at Kirby Cove, with the tide coming in fast and hard, I noticed the starfish. With an extreme wide-angle lens, it was possible to get the starfish and Golden Gate Bridge in one frame. To get enough depth of field, I used a long exposure with my tripod legs deep in the surf.

A few moments after I took the photo, this portion of the beach was under water. *(Photo on pages 40 and 41.)*

**27**

About once a month, the surf beneath the Golden Gate opposite Fort Point produces a break that locals like to surf. Riding this wave, however, takes care and courage: Paddle out too far, and the Golden Gate current will sweep you into the open Pacific. *(Photo on page 42.)*

**28**

On Baker Beach, on the San Francisco side of the Golden Gate, as late afternoon turned to evening, the Golden Gate Bridge was reflected in the surf. I used a polarizing filter to enhance the red lines of the reflection of the northern tower shown in this photo. *(Photo on pages 42 and 43.)*

The tug looked lonely in the fog and setting sun.

I watched from across the bay and wondered where it was going and what cargo the tug would guide. The foghorns in the marina called their mournful sound, and the world turned to gold as the sun set into the sea of fog. *(Photo on pages 44 and 45.)*

**29**

I took this photo from the top of Wildcat Peak in Tilden Park, looking toward the Golden Gate at sunset, and hiked back down to the Inspiration Point parking lot in the dark. *(Photo on pages 46 and 47.)*

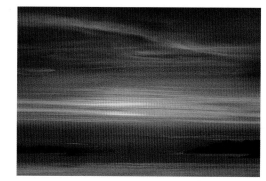

**30**

This is a more distant view from the summit of Wildcat Peak, looking toward the Golden Gate, and showing an immense and wonderful gradient in the sky. *(Photo on page 48.)*

**31**

The Golden Gate is a visual embodiment of paradox. It is not unusual to find storm and sun, clouds and strong rays of sunlight, during the same sunset—or even at the same instant. The vista is always changing.

How wonderful to bear witness to one of the greatest displays on earth! *(Photo on page 49.)*

**32**

**33**

This is a photo from the shoreline at Treasure Island, directly across from the Golden Gate.

Treasure Island juts out into San Francisco Bay. Often windy, this forlorn ex-military base has been partially converted to decaying housing stock. The dilapidated housing projects are seedy and run-down, but the vistas of the Golden Gate as you walk along the coastline are world-class. *(Photo on pages 50 and 51.)*

**34**

It rained all day, with the consistent steady rain that is typical of winter storms that blow through the Golden Gate from the Pacific. Then, in the late afternoon, the wind picked up, and the clouds started breaking up.

Sunset was a glorious show of yellows, a great relief after the day of rain. *(Photo on pages 52 and 53.)*

**35**

San Francisco and the other cities of the bay are largely built on reclaimed marsh land. The bay itself is on the migration path for many species of birds. If you wander the waterfront (like the Richmond shoreline shown here) at dusk, you'll usually see many of the birds as well as traces of the estuarine origins of the Bay Area. *(Photo on pages 54 and 55.)*

**36**

If you look closely at this photo, you can see the first lights of the Golden Gate Bridge coming on. Often, the best photos can be taken at this "between" time: between late afternoon and night, when there's still some remains of the day, and as the first lights come on. *(Photo on pages 56 and 57.)*

The fog rolls in through the Golden Gate thick, like a fleece blanket. Beneath the fog, the world is gray and overcast. But across the bay, from the peaks of the Coastal Range, the towers of the Golden Gate Bridge reach for the sunshine with joy and passion. *(Photo on pages 58 and 59.)*

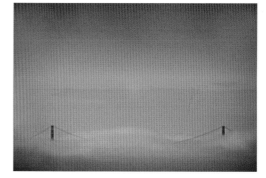

37

I took this photo from a vacant lot on upper Euclid Avenue in the Berkeley hills.

My favorite part of this photo is the long shadows cast by the southern approach to the Golden Gate Bridge in the strong light of the setting sun. *(Photo on pages 60 and 61.)*

38

It was a beautiful, sunny day on the east side of the bay. But when I climbed to a high place to photograph sunset, the Golden Gate had mostly been swallowed by the fog.

How odd to be on the sailboat, shown in the front left of this photo, sailing in the sunshine, perhaps totally unaware of the fog bank about to engulf the world. *(Photo on pages 62 and 63.)*

39

You can see "optical artifacts" on the lower right of this image. These optical artifacts are caused when light passes through internal elements of the lens. You see them most often when the camera is pointed at a strong light source, in this case the sun.

I'd normally consider the presence of optical artifacts a problem. But in this photo, I think the artifacts serve to balance the composition, and are more "feature" than "bug." *(Photo on page 63.)*

40

**41**

As I was coming home from Yosemite and a winter land of white snow, the sun was setting over the Golden Gate. I couldn't resist a photography stop, in the Oakland hills above Interstate 580, to capture this magnificent sunset. *(Photo on pages 64 and 65.)*

**42**

The sun was setting to the north of the Golden Gate Bridge in early February. As it set, the sun lit the clouds over the bridge with a wonderful, radiant light.

As I captured the scene, I thought the golden clouds formed an arch above the bridge. *(Photo on pages 66 and 67.)*

**43**

This is the southern tower of the Golden Gate Bridge, shown with a full moon rising in June.

I positioned myself along the Marin Headlands shore so that the moon lined up above the tower as it rose. *(Photo on page 69.)*

**44**

This is a photo taken from the Berkeley Pier.

Sometimes things come together, and all you have to do is stand there and press the shutter release! *(Photo on pages 70 and 71.)*

A projection of a shadow on a cloud—like the one shown in this photograph—is called a "crepuscular" effect. In this series of photos, the crepuscular shadow seems to be a second, rubber tower peeling away from the real southern Golden Gate Bridge tower. *(Photo on page 72.)*

45

The whole sequence of crepuscular effects was finished in a matter of seconds when the clouds dispersed. In other words, you had to be in the right place at exactly the right time to see this phenomenon. *(Photo on page 72.)*

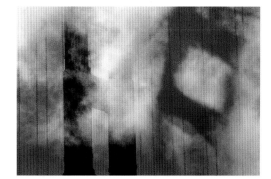

46

I took the series of photos of the bridge tower and crepuscular shadows from a sailboat close to the northern tower of the bridge, and out a short distance in San Francisco Bay. *(Photo on pages 72 and 73.)*

47

The Golden Gate Bridge sits right where the Pacific-born weather systems meet the land and the relatively warmer water of the San Francisco Bay.

I took this photograph from a deck of a sailing vessel below the bridge. The clouds were breaking up and the refraction of the sun created this alternate worldview of bridge and mist. *(Photo on page 74.)*

48

49    On a chilly, foggy day I climbed Hawk Hill with hopes that the weather might clear. After I had been standing around for a few hours trying to keep warm, the clouds lifted for a glorious light show. *(Photo on pages 75.)*

50    Climbing up to the top of Indian Rock, I looked out on a world of rain and wetness. For a moment, the storm cleared, and I took a couple photos. Then the rain came down hard again, and I had to put my camera away. *(Photo on pages 76 and 77.)*

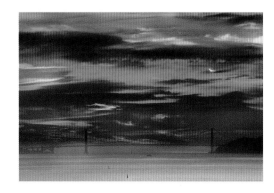

51    This photograph of the Golden Gate and surrounding bay was taken from the summit of Wildcat Peak.

Wildcat Peak is directly opposite the Golden Gate in Tilden Park in the Coastal Range. Despite several trails to the summit, it is often a lonely, serene, and deserted place, with wind whistling overhead and birds swooping by. *(Photo on pages 78 and 79.)*

52    Until the last moment, I thought this would be just another ho-hum winter sunset, with the Golden Gate cloaked in gray clouds. Then the weather broke, and the sky lit up with the fantastic colors you see in this photo. *(Photo on pages 80 and 81.)*

After days of clear, cold, wonderful winter weather, there were magnificent winter storm clouds in the sky. As the sun sank below the arc of the Pacific, it lit the clouds with colorful glory. Then the sun dipped below the horizon, and the world became cold and gray. *(Photo on page 82.)*

**53**

If you visit Lands End, below the California Palace of the Legion of Honor and Lincoln Park in San Francisco, you'll find this stone labyrinth by Eduardo Aguilera, who painstakingly created and maintains this art installation.

I photographed Aguilera's labyrinth using an extreme wide-angle lens to capture the Golden Gate Bridge in the same frame. *(Photo on page 83.)*

**54**

This is a time exposure, taken in foggy and cold conditions from Slacker Ridge. Slacker Ridge is a high point that lies directly to the north of the Golden Gate Bridge in the Marin Headlands.

The time exposure combined with the fog to create the impressionistic effects you see in this photo. *(Photo on pages 84 and 85.)*

**55**

It rained in the Bay Area for several days, flooding creeks, filling puddles, and making the world wet. Then the storm cleared, and after the storm this sunset was sweet and golden. *(Photo on pages 86.)*

**56**

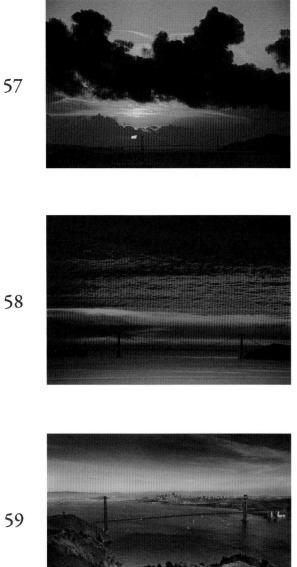

**57**

In a break in stormy weather, I photographed this series of clouds at sunset from the top of Indian Rock. *(Photo on page 87.)*

**58**

The lights of the Golden Gate Bridge just came on, and the bridge itself was silhouetted against a crimson bank of clouds, a wall of fire in the sky. *(Photo on pages 88 and 89.)*

**59**

On New Year's Day, I climbed to the top of Hawk Hill and photographed this strong, clear vista of San Francisco and the Golden Gate. *(Photo on pages 90 and 91.)*

**60**

This photo shows the Adventure Cat, a wind-powered cruise ship, tacking around the south tower of the Golden Gate Bridge.

Somehow, the Adventure Cat seems to turn up in quite a few of my Golden Gate photos. I guess she's there to watch the sunset—and so am I! *(Photo on page 93.)*

This photo shows rush-hour traffic on the Golden Gate Bridge, taken from a ridge to the southwest of Sausalito.

It was getting dark, so I set my camera for a long exposure. This turned the cars' headlights and taillights into bright white and red ribbons. *(Photo on page 94.)*

**61**

From a saddle in one of the hills behind the bridge, the northern approach to the Golden Gate Bridge took on the abstract shape of an S-curve to my eyes.

As I took this photo, the coyotes sang behind me down in Gerbode Valley, where all was dark. In front, the traffic patterns abstracted into solid streaks of yellow and red light. *(Photo on page 95.)*

**62**

Although I'd expect sunset colors to be at their best toward the west, in this photo, the sunset appears to the east across the Golden Gate and above San Francisco. Because the sun had set below the western horizon, it briefly lit parts of these clouds underneath with a wonderful pink light. *(Photo on page 96.)*

**63**

From Wildcat Peak in Tilden Park, I watched the patterns of the clouds, heavy with moisture, come and go in the wind. I could watch this scenery and movement forever! *(Photo on pages 96 and 97.)*

**64**

**65** There's a steady flow of shipping passing in and out of the Golden Gate. Most of these tankers and container ships are coming from or going to Asia. I photographed this tanker passing under the Golden Gate Bridge from the abandoned fortifications along the Marin Headlands shore of the Golden Gate. *(Photo on pages 98 and 99.)*

**66** Looking down at Kirby Cove from an old, ruined battery on the cliff side, I could see that the high tide had covered Kirby Beach.

In the upper part of the photo, the lights and shadows of the Golden Gate Bridge roadway helped create an interesting composition. *(Photo on pages 100 and 101.)*

**67** From beneath the Golden Gate Bridge, the towers and roadway stretch elegantly toward the sky. *(Photo on page 102.)*

**68** On the San Francisco side of the Golden Gate, the shore is rugged and windswept. Along the Golden Gate beaches, views of the bridge crop up incongruously.

This photo was taken from the ruins overlooking the old Russian baths. *(Photo on page 103.)*

As golden afternoon light streamed down, I took this photo of a sailboat cruising the Golden Gate from the deck of a catamaran sailing the bay. *(Photo on page 104.)*

69

Marin Headlands, part of the Golden Gate National Recreation Area, is an astounding wilderness for one so close to a major city. At night, the coyotes wail, and by day you could be in the middle of nowhere.

You can tell you're not in the wilderness because the city and the towers of the Golden Gate *will* peek over the hills. The northern bridge tower is shown here from Wolf Ridge Trail, looking back and across Gerbode Valley. *(Photo on page 105.)*

70

On my way up from a sunset vigil on Kirby Cove, I stopped at Battery Spencer to make a long exposure of the Golden Gate Bridge at night. *(Photo on pages 106 and 107.)*

71

From Hawk Hill, the lights of San Francisco and the Golden Gate Bridge made a festive display. Long trails created by the running lights of airplanes in motion added to the effect. *(Photo on page 108.)*

72

**73**  It had rained heavily over night, and the path around Battery Spencer in the Marin Headlands was filled with puddles. I photographed the Golden Gate Bridge looking over Battery Spencer, and made sure to include this reflection in the puddle for the sake of symmetry. *(Photo on page 109.)*

**74**  I took this photo from a short distance down the trail to Point Bonita. I like the way the photo shows early spring daffodils, the moon setting, and the Golden Gate Bridge, all in one frame. *(Photo on pages 110 and 111.)*

**75**  From Hawk Hill, on a crisp spring day, the Golden Gate Bridge and the city looked hyper-real, so beautiful that the view made me feel glad to be alive. *(Photo on pages 112 and 113.)*

**76**  From above Bonita Cove, Black Sands Beach stretches to meet Point Diablo, with the Golden Gate Bridge and San Francisco behind. *(Photo on page 114.)*

This photo shows a full summer moon, known as a "rose moon," rising over the city of San Francisco from across the Golden Gate.

As the foghorns blew their diatonic notes, I especially enjoyed the diaphanous quality of the clouds. Sometimes partial revelation is more exciting than seeing the whole thing. *(Photo on page 115.)*

77

From Muir Beach Overlook, you can see south along the Marin Headlands, the outer opening of the Golden Gate, and beyond the Golden Gate to the lights of South San Francisco.

I carefully trod the narrow ledge out to the overlook in the dark, and took this photo to emphasize the colors in the clouds, which reflect the lights of the city and the last light of sunset. *(Photo on page 116.)*

78

The narrow span of the Golden Gate Bridge retains its elegance as cars pass through the dusk. Often, the bridge has more light, later than surrounding areas—so it tends to stand out in contrast to the background landscape. *(Photo on page 117.)*

79

If you happen to be on the deck of a ship passing under the Golden Gate Bridge, and look up, it's likely you will see these girders. They are part of the support system of the bridge, and your view will be of this engineering underpinning, rather than the massive, soaring towers. *(Photo on page 118.)*

80

**81**

On one of the tower stanchions below the bridge, the shadow of the girders makes an interesting abstract pattern. *(Photo on page 118.)*

**82**

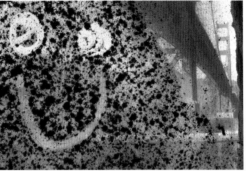

When I was visiting Fort Point, there was construction going on overhead, on the southern side of the Golden Gate Bridge.

High on the topmost tier of the old batteries, the windows in the crenelations were either boarded over, or covered on the outside with dust and debris. Someone had managed to climb a ladder up the walls of the old fort to make their mark in the dust outside this window. *(Photo on pages 118 and 119.)*

**83**

After walking a couple of miles along the Coastal Trail in the dark, I turned and saw this view of the Golden Gate and San Francisco from a low saddle. I guessed at the exposure, and was pleased to see the motion trails when I looked at the photo at a large size. *(Photo on pages 120 and 121.)*

**84**

On Indian Rock, there were no clouds but plenty of crowds enjoying a weekend sunset. The only place I could find to set up my tripod, considering the crowded conditions, was at the very pinnacle of the rock.

I made a great effort to concentrate as I took this photo, because I was on a very small ledge, and a fall would have taken me down 40 or 50 feet. *(Photo on pages 122 and 123.)*

The most interesting thing to me about this photo of the full moon aligned over the south Golden Gate Bridge tower is the way the moon has retained its fully saturated coloration, while the landscape tends toward the black of night. *(Photo on page 125.)*

 85

Sunset came early and fast while I was making this wintertime photo from the Marin Headlands. With darkness falling so swiftly, I had to hurry to capture the clarity of the light. *(Photo on pages 126 and 127.)*

86

This photo, taken from the rocky shore of Treasure Island, shows an interesting composition of the sun, Golden Gate Bridge, and a single sailboat. *(Photo on page 128.)*

 87

This is a photo of the sun setting to the south of the Golden Gate Bridge from the waterfront in Cesar Chavez Park in Berkeley. There are only a few days in January in which the sun appears to set to the south of the bridge from this location. *(Photo on page 129.)*

 88

**89**

The optical artifact you can see to the right of the Golden Gate in this photo is caused by internal flaring in the lens.

On the whole, I think the golden light and the lens flare compliment each other in this composition. *(Photo on page 130.)*

**90**

This photo demonstrates an optical phenomenon called "double refraction" or "birefringence." In double refraction, each ray of light separates into two rays (the "ordinary" ray and the "extraordinary" ray) when the light heads through the lens. The extra suns in my photo are caused by the extraordinary rays. The birefringence effect is dependent on how the light is polarized, so I used a polarizing filter to position one of the sun "echoes" on the north bridge tower. *(Photo on page 131.)*

**91**

For me, this photo is about the incredibly intense red of this Golden Gate sunset against the stability of the Marin Headlands and the rectilinear shape of the bridge. *(Photo on page 132.)*

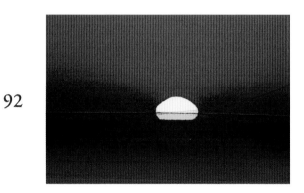

**92**

If you watch the setting sun carefully as it heads for the horizon, you'll see that the sun moves sideways as well as downward.

I had gone to the same spot for nearly a month, waiting for the sun to go down near the center of the bridge. Finally, my patience was rewarded when the sun slid down and sideways and set almost exactly in the center of the Golden Gate Bridge span. *(Photo on page 133.)*

This is a photo of the beach at Kirby Cove with the tide most of the way out. You can see a small creek running across the beach, and the night lights of the Golden Gate Bridge and San Francisco. *(Photo on pages 134 and 135.)*

93

On the beach at Kirby Cove, as the day faded to the soft, pink lights of sunset, I experimented with capturing the motion of the tide coming in across the sand. *(Photo on page 136.)*

94

From Horseshoe Bay near Sausalito, you can look south and west toward the Golden Gate Bridge, shown here after sunset with the fog rolling in. *(Photo on pages 136 and 137.)*

95

The thing that intrigues me most about this view of the Golden Gate Bridge in the twilight is the way the bridge, the bridge's shadow, and the light from the bridge all appear to converge toward a point near the south tower. *(Photo on page 138.)*

96

97

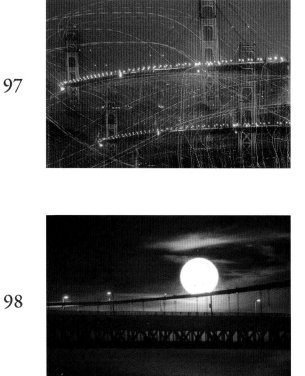

I was photographing well after sunset at Baker Beach on the San Francisco side of the Golden Gate. My tripod legs were in the surf. Suddenly, in the middle of an exposure, a large wave came along.

I grabbed my camera and tripod and ran for shore, putting the tripod down on dry sand. When the exposure completed, I saw I had an interesting, if unplanned, multiple exposure image. *(Photo on page 139.)*

98

In this view from Kirby Cove, the moon rose and touched the Golden Gate Bridge. For a brief instant, the moon seemed to rest on the suspension lines of the bridge itself. *(Photo on page 140.)*

99

As the bright summer moon emerged from behind the San Francisco skyline, a cruise ship passed in front. I used a moderate telephoto lens to isolate the moon and ship beneath the Golden Gate Bridge, and to tell the story of the ship in motion and the full moon. *(Photo on page 141.)*

100

This is a true night photo of the Golden Gate Bridge, taken from the west of Battery Spencer.

I like the way the bridge casts a golden reflection in the water, making the scene truly the "Golden Gate." *(Photo on pages 142 and 143.)*

Point Bonita marks the north side of the opening to the Golden Gate. From Point Bonita, the lights of the Golden Gate Bridge and San Francisco twinkled around the bend.

What was the mystery boat in the moonlight? A fishing trawler perhaps, or a Coast Guard ship waiting? The lights of an old farmhouse (now Golden Gate National Recreation Area employee housing) look warm and inviting, and surprisingly rural, so close to San Francisco. *(Photo on pages 144 and 145.)*

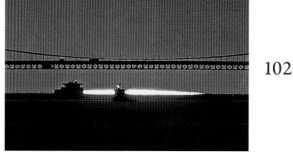

101

The lights on the tug seem to echo the setting sun, as the day goes down in orange behind the Golden Gate Bridge. *(Photo on pages 146 and 147.)*

102

From beneath the Golden Gate Bridge, the girders covered with thousands of rivets seem to form a gigantic letter X. *(Photo on page 148.)*

103

In the winter, the setting sun migrates south along the Pacific, and returns north following the solstice. The mathematics and angles are a bit complex—things depend upon the position of the observer as well as the relationship of sun and bridge. For a day in early February, one can see—and photograph—the sun behind the bridge span between the towers, provided the weather is clear at sunset. *(Photo on back cover.)*

104

## Dedication

To our Golden Gate boys:
Julian, Nicky, and Mathew

## Acknowledgments

Special thanks to Mark Brokering, Roslyn Bullas, Martin Davis, Virginia Davis, Eva Dienel, Jennifer Durning, Veronica Haas, Dr. Michael Katz, Laura Keresty, Eliza Schwindt, Rick Smolan, Matt Wagner, Emily White, and Caroline Winnett.

## Colophon

The photos in this book were created in RAW format using Nikon digital Single Lens Reflex cameras and lenses ranging from a 10.5mm digital fisheye to a 400mm telephoto. Most photos were taken using a Gitzo tripod with a Kirk ballhead.

The photos were processed on a dual-core Intel Xeon Mac using Adobe Bridge, Adobe Photoshop CS2, and Adobe Photoshop CS3.

Text for the book was set using Adobe Garamond Premier Pro. Book layout and design were created using Adobe InDesign CS2.

*100 Views of the Golden Gate* was printed in ShenZhen, China, through Asia Pacific Offset, Inc, using a Komori press on acid-free 140gsm Gold East Gloss Art paper.